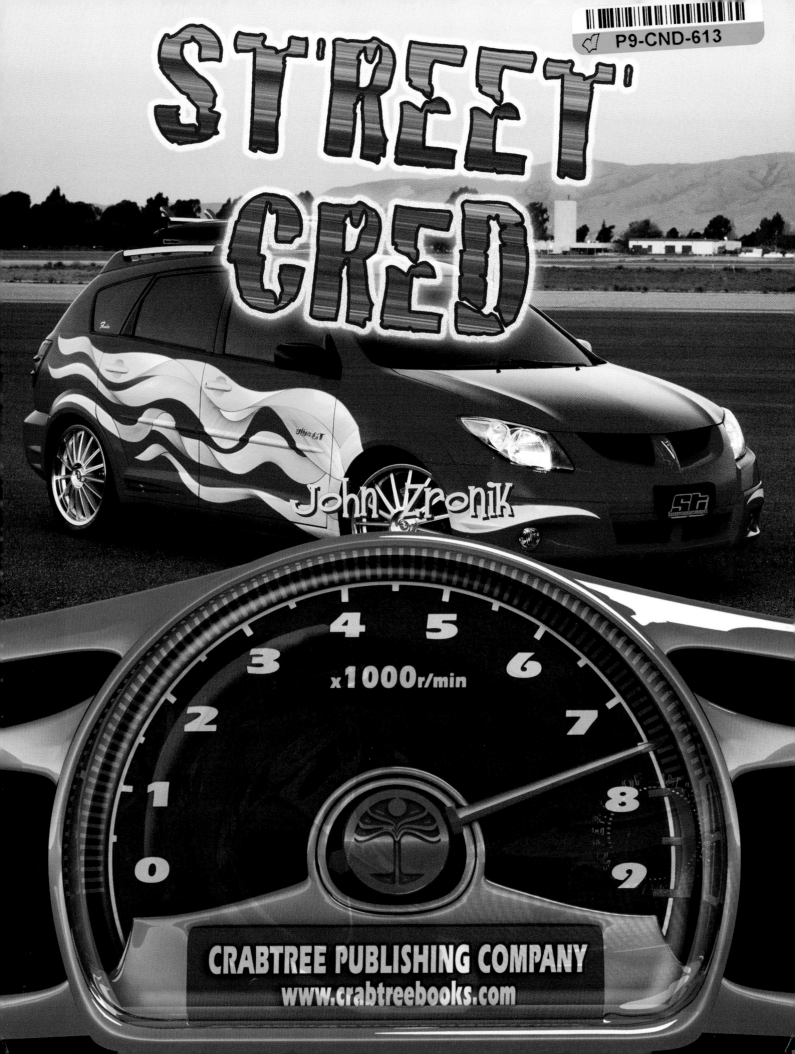

STREET CRED

John Zronik

x1000r/min

CRABTREE PUBLISHING COMPANY
www.crabtreebooks.com

Crabtree Publishing Company
www.crabtreebooks.com

For wee Ewan, and the road ahead of us. Love mummy
Dedicated by Rose Gowsell

Coordinating editor: Ellen Rodger
Series editor: Rachel Eagen
Project editor: Adrianna Morganelli
Editors: Carrie Gleason, L. Michelle Nielsen
Design and production coordinator: Rosie Gowsell
Production assistance: Samara Parent
Art direction: Rob MacGregor
Scanning technician: Arlene Arch-Wilson
Photo research: Allison Napier

Consultant: Andrew Elliot

Photo Credits: Rodolfo Arpia/Alamy: p. 25 (bottom); Transtock Inc./Alamy: p. 15 (bottom); AP/Wide World Photos: p. 13 (bottom), p. 21 (bottom), p. 23 (bottom), p. 24, p. 31 (bottom); Luca Babini/Corbis: p. 4; Gene Blevins/LA Daily News/Corbis: p. 23 (top); Bettmann/Corbis: p. 8 (bottom); Rick Friedman/Corbis: p. 9 (bottom); Robert Galbraith/Reuters/Corbis: p. 28 (top); Axel Koester/

Corbis: p. 28 (bottom); George D. Lepp/Corbis: p. 17 (bottom); Reuters/Corbis: p. 19 (bottom); Ted Soqui/Corbis: p. 10, p. 11 (bottom); Katy Winn/Corbis: p. 29 (bottom), p. 30; Courtesy of the Detroit News: p. 8 (top); Orlando/Getty Images: p. 7 (bottom); Joe Raedle/Getty Images: p. 18 (bottom); Dan Callister/Online USA/Getty Images: p. 29 (top); Joe Sohm/The Image Works: p. 6; Ron Kimball/Ron Kimball Stock: cover, p. 1, p. 5 (bottom), p. 7 (top), p. 9 (top), p. 11 (top, middle), p. 12 (both), p. 13 (top), p. 14, p. 15 (top), p. 17 (top), p. 18 (top), p. 19 (top), p. 20, p. 21 (top), p. 22, p. 25 (top), p. 26 (both), p. 27 (bottom); Greg Smith/photoillustrators.com: p. 31 (top). Other images stock photo CD.

Cover: Tuners are sport compact cars that have been modified to reach greater speeds. The Honda Civic is a popular car among tuner enthusiasts.

Title page: One of the most popular designs that car customizers paint on the bodies of cars are flames.

Library and Archives Canada Cataloguing in Publication

Zronik, John Paul, 1972-
   Street cred / John Zronik.
(Automania!)
Includes index.
ISBN-13: 978-0-7787-3006-4 (bound)
ISBN-10: 0-7787-3006-9 (bound)
ISBN-13: 978-0-7787-3028-6 (pbk.)
ISBN-10: 0-7787-3028-X (pbk.)

   1. Automobiles--Juvenile literature. 2. Automobiles--Customizing--Juvenile literature. 3. Automobiles--Decoration--Juvenile literature. I. Title. II. Series.

TL255.2.Z76 2006   j629.222   C2006-902459-6

Library of Congress Cataloging-in-Publication Data

Zronik, John Paul, 1972-
   Street cred / written by John Zronik.
      p. cm. -- (Automania!)
   Includes index.
   ISBN-13: 978-0-7787-3006-4 (rlb)
   ISBN-10: 0-7787-3006-9 (rlb)
   ISBN-13: 978-0-7787-3028-6 (pbk)
   ISBN-10: 0-7787-3028-X (pbk)
   1. Automobiles--Customizing--Juvenile literature. I. Title. II. Series.
   TL255.2.Z76 2006
   629.28'72--dc22
                                                      2006014365

Crabtree Publishing Company

www.crabtreebooks.com   1-800-387-7650

Published in Canada
Crabtree Publishing
616 Welland Ave.
St. Catharines, ON
L2M 5V6

Published in the United States
Crabtree Publishing
PMB16A
350 Fifth Ave., Suite 3308
New York, NY 10118

Published in the United Kingdom
Crabtree Publishing
White Cross Mills
High Town, Lancaster
LA1 4XS

Published in Australia
Crabtree Publishing
386 Mt. Alexander Rd.
Ascot Vale (Melbourne)
VIC 3032

Contents

All the Rage   4

Setting Trends   6

Lowriders   10

Hot Rodding   12

Tuned for Speed   14

Cool Customs   16

Car Accessories   20

Hot Wheels   22

Car Audio   24

Brushing on Style   26

Celebrity Car Culture   28

Behind the Machines   30

Glossary and Index   32

All the Rage

Cars that have street credibility, or street cred, are considered "cool" within street culture, or the culture on the streets of cities and towns. Street cred means that the vehicles are modified, or changed, to be stylish and driven fast. Street cred also includes expensive cars that only wealthy people can afford.

A Way of Life

Street cred car culture began in California during the late 1930s and spread across the United States. Today, expensive modifications and additions are made to cars, such as new wheels and stereo systems, to make the owners appear wealthier and flashier on the street. Many car owners display their cars' street cred by cruising, or driving slowly down busy streets. Other people race dangerously down city streets in cars that have been modified to drive fast.

Cruising city streets is a popular way to show off a car. Many people cruise in lowriders, which are cars that ride close to the ground.

Street Cred Cars

Some car models are designed in factories to have street credibility, such as Lamborghinis. Many regular passenger cars, trucks, and **sport utility vehicles**, or SUVs, are **customized** to change the way they look or to enhance their performance. Custom cars are created with aftermarket parts, which are parts that are added to cars after they have been built by a manufacturer. Hot rods and tuners are examples of fast street cred cars. A hot rod is a car that has been modified to drive fast. They are usually classic cars from the 1920s and 1930s. Tuners are sport compact cars that have been modified for greater speed and a stylish appearance. Sport compact cars are smaller than regular, or mid-sized, passenger cars and they have **front-wheel drive**.

Street cred car owners gain popularity and acceptance within car communities for having the fastest or most eye-catching vehicles. The Toyota Supra is a popular tuner car because its powerful engine requires few modifications to increase the car's speed.

(above) Many owners of street cred cars join auto clubs and attend car events, such as contests, shows, and races. The Grand National Roadster Show in the United States is an event where hot rods are displayed to the public.

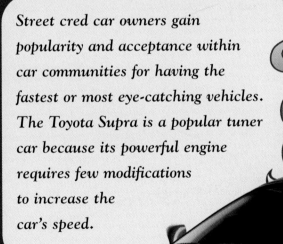

setting trends

The characteristics of each type of street cred car are as distinct as their histories. Cool car culture began in California during the 1930s, and spread throughout the United States over the years to follow.

Lowriders

The lowrider culture originated among the Mexican American community in Los Angeles, California, in the late 1930s. The community developed its own style by lowering vehicles to ride close to the ground. Sometimes, just the back end of the car was lowered. Many Mexican American teenagers created lowriders by modifying used, inexpensive car models, such as Fords and Chevrolets. Cultural and religious symbols were often painted on car bodies, and custom wheels and **hubcaps** were added. Teenagers cruised in their lowriders through Mexican American neighborhoods, called *barrios*, to show off. By the late 1950s, lowriders were cruised down the main strip in Los Angeles.

Creating lowriders was a popular trend among Mexican American teenagers in the late 1930s. They also developed their own street slang, and wore distinct hair and clothing styles, such as the zoot suit, shown in this mural in Los Angeles, California. The zoot suit was an oversized suit with a long knee-length jacket and baggy pants.

6

California Hot Rod Culture

The hot rod culture formed in California in 1945 when World War II ended. World War II was an international conflict that lasted from 1939 to 1945. During the war, people had less money to buy luxury items, which caused car sales to drop. Sports cars were too expensive for average American teenagers to purchase, so many teens created their own sports cars by building hot rods. Hot rods were built using inexpensive cars from the 1920s and 1930s, such as models made by Ford, Chevrolet, Dodge, and Mercury. The engines were replaced with new engines, or were tuned, or modified, to give them more power. Wide tires were also added for better grip on the road. To help the car go faster, owners reduced car weights by removing parts such as bumpers, windshields, fenders, roofs, and hoods. Teenagers raced their hot rods on **salt flats** and drag strips, which are straight stretches of road.

(below) Hot rods were painted bright colors to attract attention. Many hot rods had designs painted on them, such as flames.

(above) Hot rods were built for racing. Drivers wait for the flag to drop and the race to begin across the ice at Lily Pond, New Hampshire.

Detroit: The Cruising Era

Detroit, Michigan, was the top automobile producer in the United States after World War II. As a result, cruising in American-made cars became a popular pastime among Detroit teenagers during the 1950s and 1960s. Ford **coupes**, Mustangs, and Dodges were popular cruising cars. Teenagers waxed their vehicles to a bright shine, removed hubcaps, and purchased **vanity license plates** to attract attention. Teens slowly drove their cars up and down Woodward Avenue, the most popular street to cruise in Detroit. They stopped at drive-in restaurants, diners, and parking lots to meet other people their age. Some teens participated in drag races on city streets.

(above) The cruising era is remembered as an important part of Detroit's automotive history. Woodward Avenue was a favorite spot for racing and cruising.

Teens often took a break from cruising Woodward Avenue by stopping at drive-in restaurants. Wearing trendy clothes and listening to popular music of the day were other important aspects of cruising.

(right) Tuners are raced on tracks, as well as on city streets. The engine of this 1997 Honda Civic has been tuned to increase the car's speed.

Tuner Culture

Tuner culture originated in Japan, where teenagers raced on streets in Tokyo in sport compact cars. They tuned the engines to increase their cars' power and speed. The North American tuner scene began in Los Angeles, California, in the early 1990s. The engines of cars **imported** into the United States were modified to drive faster. Most of the cars imported from other countries were from Japan. Japanese car models, such as Honda, Nissan, Acura, and Mazda became popular tuner cars among American teenagers. Early tuners were often raced in street races and drag racing events. By the late 1990s, the tuner scene had spread from Los Angeles to other cities across the United States.

(below) Drag races are dangerous and often illegal. Drivers risk their own lives and the lives of other people on the road. Here drivers wait for the signal to start a race on a road. If caught, they could spend time in jail.

Lowriders

Lowriders have grown in popularity among car enthusiasts since the late 1930s. Today, cars that cruise "slow and low" give their owners instant street cred.

Going Low

A lowrider is a car or truck that has been lowered so the vehicle's body is close to the ground. A vehicle is lowered by altering its suspension, which is a system of springs and **axles** that support the car's weight. Rough roads and obstacles, such as speed bumps, make driving lowriders difficult. **Hydraulic** suspension systems help avoid scraping the bottom of lowriders against the road. These systems allow drivers to adjust the height of their vehicles. Hydraulic systems are also used to make one end or side of a car bounce completely off the ground. Some lowriders can bounce up to six feet (1.8 meters) into the air!

Popular Lowrider Models

The cars used to make lowriders must have **frames** that can support the hydraulic suspension. The 1964 Chevrolet Impala is the most common choice for lowriders. Many models from the 1970s and 1980s are becoming popular, such as the Chevrolet Monte Carlo and the Oldsmobile Cutlass. Today, import cars made by companies including Honda, Nissan, Acura, and Toyota are used to create lowriders. The most popular models include the Honda Civic, the Nissan RX7, and the Acura Infinity. Small truck models of various years manufactured by Mazda, Ford, Dodge, and Nissan are also modified into lowriders.

A lowrider community still exists today. The 1964 Chevrolet Impala is still one of the most popular cars for lowriding.

Adding Some Flash

Lowriders are often customized to look cool and to improve their performance. Accessories such as loud stereo systems, interior lights, custom hubcaps and steering wheels, and tires with gold- or **chrome**-spoked wheels may be added to lowriders to give them extra street cred. In many lowriders, the seat **upholstery** is custom-made with leather, **tweed**, or velvet. Sometimes, neon lights are installed beneath lowriders that illuminate when the car is driven at night. Many coats of paint are often applied to lowriders to create bright, shiny finishes. Some owners choose custom paint jobs for their lowriders, including designs such as flames, scallops, and stripes.

(top and above) Gold- or chrome-spoked wheels are popular features of lowriders.

The custom interior of this lowrider gives the car and its owner extra street cred.

Hot Rodding

Hot rods are built for speed and modified for style. Today, modern and classic hot rods are displayed at auto shows across North America, and are driven on city streets for enjoyment.

Popular Hot Rods

Over time, certain car models have been more popular than others for building hot rods. In the 1930s, cars built by Ford were used for hot rod modification. Later, Chevrolets from the 1950s were used. Dodge Chargers, Mercurys, and Ford Mustangs also became popular models for hot rodding. Import cars are becoming popular hot rods now. These models include the Mazdaspeed Protege and the Honda Civic. Today, many cars are designed in the factory to look and be driven like hot rods. Cars such as the Plymouth Prowler and the Chrysler PT Cruiser require little modification because they already have sleek bodies and powerful engines.

Hot Rod Evolution

In the early days of hot rodding, teenagers transformed affordable cars into racing hot rods by replacing or tuning their engines. They removed heavy car parts to reduce weight so that their hot rods went even faster. Today, many car companies manufacture lightweight car parts, such as body panels, fenders, and bumpers. These parts can be added to hot rods without slowing their speed while they are driven on streets or raced on tracks.

The Plymouth Prowler (above) and Chrysler PT Cruiser (left) are popular hot rods today.

Customizing Rods

Hot rod owners customize their cars to suit their individual tastes. Many people install custom tires, headlights, taillights, and exhaust pipes in their hot rods. Inside, owners add customized seat covers, floor mats, and knobs for the cars' **gearshifts**. Some hot rods have open engines, meaning the engines are not covered by a hood, and are visible from the outside. Hot rods are custom painted and many owners add **decals** to their cars' bodies. Decal stickers are printed with designs, such as the owner's favorite sports team, or the number of a favorite race car driver.

(above) This hot rod's interior has been customized with red and white leather.

(below) Hundreds of hot rods are lined up before they are displayed in a parade at the York Expo Center in York, Pennsylvania.

Rod Racing

In the 1940s, teens raced their hot rods on city streets. To discourage teens from this dangerous pastime, an organization called the National Hot Rod Association (NHRA) was founded in California in 1951. The NHRA oversees legal drag racing events in North America. The races, called the U.S. Nationals, take place in the summer and winter of each year. There are different series of drag races for different types of vehicles. In a drag race, two cars race down specially designed drag strips from a stopped position to a finish line. The driver that crosses the finish line first wins the race. The drag strips range in length, but the most common distance is one quarter of a mile (0.4 km).

Tuned for speed

Tuners are sport compact cars that have been upgraded and modified to increase their speed. Most tuners are imported, but North American cars are starting to gain popularity for tuner modification today.

Tuner Types

Many tuners are made by modifying Japanese sport compact cars, manufactured by companies such as Honda, Mitsubishi, Nissan, and Toyota. These companies have begun to manufacture cars with engines that have already been tuned. Pre-tuned cars include the Honda Civic Si, the Mazda3, and the Toyota Corolla XRS. Today, many North American car manufacturers are building sport compact cars designed for engine tuning. Ford was the first North American manufacturer to build a car specifically for tuner fans. The model was called the Ford Focus ZX5. Many companies also manufacture aftermarket parts, such as **superchargers**, that can be added to cars to increase performance.

Spoilers are fitted to racing tuners to help prevent the cars from lifting off of the road while traveling at high speeds.

Racing Tuners

Many people illegally race tuners on city streets. They usually race at night on public roads that are not busy, to avoid the police. Track racing is the legal form of racing for tuner enthusiasts. The National Hot Rod Association holds tuner races at tracks across the United States each year. The races take place on specially designed drag strips made of concrete or asphalt, which are usually one quarter of a mile (0.4 kilometers) long.

Cosmetic

Aftermarket parts are added to many tuners to give them visual appeal. Some tuners are fitted with large custom wheels, loud stereo systems, and over-sized spoilers. Wheel rims made of chrome are also popular additions. A rim is the outer part of a car's wheel that is attached to the tire. Like hot rods, many tuners are painted in bright colors, and have decals on their bodies.

The Honda Civic is one of the most popular cars among tuner fans.

Enhancing Performance

Tuners raced by teams are modified with special attention to aerodynamics, or the way air flows beneath, around, and over a car. Spoilers, which are horizontal devices fitted to the back ends of cars, create downward pressure that increases tire traction, or grip, on the road. This helps the cars handle better on tight corners and gives drivers more control of their cars. Traction is also increased by using ground effects kits. A ground effects kit includes parts that are installed beneath a car's body and around its wheels, and forces the air above and beneath the car downward, making it easier for drivers to take corners at high speeds. Racing tuners have small computers that control how their engines function. Drivers use the computers to alter the amount of fuel flowing through their engines, allowing cars to go faster.

(top) Racing tuners are modified to drive fast. One way is to spray a gas called nitrous oxide, which is stored in a canister, into the engine. This releases extra oxygen, causing the fuel to burn faster, and the engine to generate more power and speed.

15

Cool Customs

Many street cred cars are customized to make them look and drive differently than other cars on the road. Owners of customized cars take pride in showing off their one-of-a-kind vehicles.

What is a Custom Car?

Custom cars are created by taking vehicles apart and rebuilding them in ways that make them look very different from the originals. This is done with aftermarket parts, or by modifying the cars' original parts. No two customized cars are alike. Some cars are fully customized, which means that all of their parts are removed, and new or reshaped parts are used to rebuild the cars on their body frames. Other times, a car's body shape and other parts are left as they are, and a custom paint job is applied to its body for a new look.

The custom paint job of this car gives it a stylish appearance.

Bodywork

Some car owners choose to customize their vehicles themselves because they are knowledgeable about cars and enjoy doing the work. Other owners hire professionals to do the work for them. An artist draws a picture of what the car's owner wants the car to look like. Sometimes, a small clay model is made to show what the car will look like after it has been customized. Auto body specialists and metal workers remove the car's body, and reshape it to create the desired look. The car's body is then put back together. Specialty mechanics, who are experts on building and repairing vehicles, improve the car's performance. This is achieved by tuning and repairing the car's mechanical parts, such as the engine and **transmission**.

(above) This car's bodywork has been fully customized.

(below) An auto body worker customizes a car by working on its body.

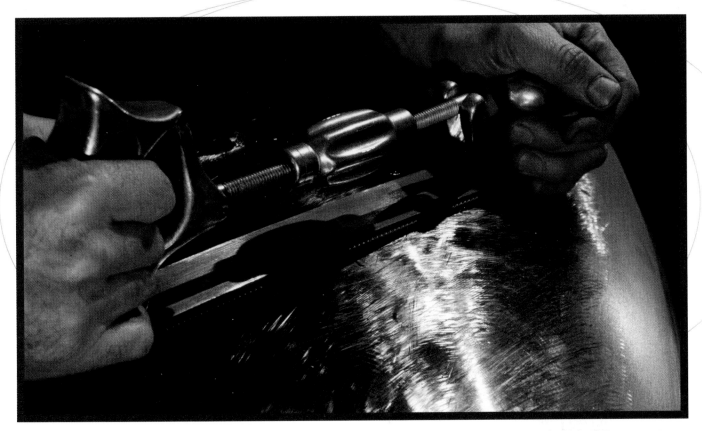

Cosmetic Customs

After the vehicle has been rebuilt, aftermarket parts are added to the car. Some parts are bolted onto the car's body. These parts include spoilers and fins, which are devices shaped like fish fins that are mounted to a car's rear. Grilles, which are grates made of metal bars, are bolted to the front ends of cars. Other aftermarket parts include wheels, headlight covers, and dashboards. Some owners choose to tint, or darken, their cars' windows. Cars are custom painted and artists paint designs and images on the cars' bodies. Decals and **magnetic** stickers are also applied.

(above) Adding fins to back ends of cars helps give them street cred.

Many custom car owners enter their cars in glow-off competitions, where lighting accessories are judged. Prizes are awarded to the owners of the cars with the best interior and exterior lighting.

Some cars undergo outrageous custom work, such as this car inspired by American singer and actor Elvis Presley.

Crazy Customs

Some cars are customized to the extreme. Some outrageous custom work is featured on the television program, *Monster Garage*. Mechanics and auto body specialists on the program have made spectacular modifications, such as transforming vehicles into dump trucks, lawn mowers, and some have even been customized to resemble animals. Some customizers create vehicles that can be driven by modifying amusement park bumper cars and golf carts.

"Dream Cars"

Concept cars, nicknamed "dream cars," are made by car manufacturers using the latest designs and technology. Most concept cars are not produced for sale to the public. They are built for display at auto shows to measure the public's reaction to them, so that car manufacturers might add some of the features to their cars in the future. Some concept car designs are based on the work of customizers. Other times, customizers get ideas for cars they are working on from concept cars.

Honda displays their concept car, called "Sprocket," in Tokyo, Japan.

Car Accessories

Thousands of different car accessories are available to make cars more comfortable and enjoyable to drive. Some accessories are added to cars to enhance their appearance, while others enhance their performance.

Soft Goods

Car accessories that do not affect a car's driving performance are known as soft goods. These accessories add visual appeal or flare to a car. Soft good options include custom upholstery in different colors and patterns, personalized embroidery on seats, and custom floor mats and steering wheel covers. High-tech soft good options include flat-panel televisions, compact disk, or CD, and DVD players, video game systems, and high-quality stereos. Some car owners even install pool tables inside their vehicles, or coffee makers and mini refrigerators inside their dashboards.

In 1997, German car manufacturer Mercedes-Benz introduced a luxury concept car called the Mercedes-Benz Maybach. The Maybach featured many soft goods, including reclining rear seats, an entertainment center, and a bar for hot and cold beverages.

Functional Accessories

Many cool car accessories have a function, or purpose. Global positioning systems, or GPSs, located on the dashboard, show drivers their positions on the road. They also provide maps and the best routes to reach their destinations. Some cars are equipped with computers that drivers can use to contact help in case of an emergency. Interior lights are available in a variety of colors to give a vehicle a cool look. They also provide light when it is needed inside a vehicle. Functional exterior lights are added to the front end of cars. They increase visibility by shining light on the road, but their size, color, and shape can also give a vehicle street cred.

A global positioning system is a cool accessory with a function.

Many car owners add "soft goods" to their vehicles for a cool look and extra street cred. This Chevrolet SSR pickup truck is equipped with a barbecue grill for cooking food. It is also furnished with a 32-inch (82-centimeter) screen and satellite television.

Hot Wheels

Adding a new set of wheels to a car is one of the easiest ways to customize a vehicle. Wheel rims and tires are important features of a street cred car, because they affect the car's appearance and driving performance.

Burning Rubber

Wheels are made in a variety of sizes and styles. Today, large wheels between 18 and 22 inches (46 and 56 centimeters) in diameter are popular. They are commonly made of aluminum **alloy**. Tires are usually made of rubber, and are fitted around the metal rims that surround a car's wheels. They have different treads, or patterns, each affecting the tires' traction on the road differently. Wide tires are popular with car owners who want their cars to look very powerful. Many racing cars are fitted with larger wheels and wide tires because they improve a car's handling.

Custom tires, such as these white-wall tires, are fitted to cars' wheels for a cool look. White-wall tires have circular, white stripes along their outsides. They have to be washed often to keep road debris and brake dust from staining them.

Stylin' Rims

A rim is the outer part of a car's wheel that the tire is fitted to. Many car owners replace their cars' stock rims with custom rims of different designs. Stock rims are installed on a car at the factory where they are made. Rims are made from solid billets, or chunks, of metal, and are often painted or **plated** with chrome to prevent them from tarnishing. The "spinner" rim is a popular tire rim within the hip-hop community. A spinner rim is made up of a separate piece of metal that spins separately from the rest of the wheel. When the car is stopped, the rims continue to spin, which makes the car appear to be still moving.

Asanti Wheels manufacture jewel encrusted wheel rims, which cost $1 million to purchase. The company offered to give away a free 2006 Bentley car to anyone who bought four rims.

Music artist Sean "P. Diddy" Combs is known for his collection of cool cars. Combs has introduced a line of custom aluminum rims, called Sean John Wheels, for sports trucks, SUVs, and luxury automobiles. Each rim costs between $700 and $3,000.

Car Audio

A cool sound system can give a vehicle street cred. The larger the system, and louder and clearer the sound, the more street cred a vehicle has. Some sound systems are loud enough to shake a car's windows!

Audio Equipment

Stock audio systems refer to the systems that car manufacturers install in cars when they are built. Many stock audio systems are made up of a radio and a tape or CD player. Today, many car owners add aftermarket sound systems to customize their cars. These include CD changers, which are systems located in the dashboard or in the trunk that hold multiple compact disks. MP3 players, which are devices that store, organize, and play **digital** music files, can be plugged into a car's dashboard. CD and MP3 players send signals to an amplifier, which is a device used to power car audio systems. The signals then travel from the amplifier to speakers.

Speakers

High-tech speakers can be installed in vehicles for exceptional sound quality and loud volume. Different types of speakers are used to create different sound effects. A subwoofer is a large speaker that creates low bass sounds. When the audio system's volume is turned up high, the low bass sounds vibrate the car. Subwoofers are installed in trunks of cars because they are too large to fit in the dashboards. A tweeter is a small speaker that produces high-pitched sounds. They are often installed inside a car's doors.

A Toyota employee demonstrates how to plug an MP3 player into the Aygo model.

Subwoofer speakers can produce high sound levels inside a vehicle. Very high sound levels can cause hearing loss if people are exposed to them for long periods of time.

(below) Many car clubs hold competitions where audio systems are judged. Car stereo enthusiasts compete to produce the loudest and clearest sounds.

Brushing on style

Artists play an important role in creating cars with street cred. Custom paint jobs may be subtle, or bold and flashy, but all great paint jobs attract attention.

Paint

Customizing vehicles has been a popular pastime among car enthusiasts since the 1950s. During this time, custom painters experimented with paint to create new colors, some of which are still used today. Paints that contain flakes of metal give cars a shiny finish, and pearlescent colors provide cars with a pearl-like sheen. Some early customizers painted cars with matte, or dull paint, which resulted in a **suede**-like finish. Gray was a popular color. This effect is still popular today, but black matte paint is more common. One paint style that gives cars a metallic finish is called "candy". Candy paint jobs involve putting a clear coat of paint on top of a silver or gold base coat. Car customizer Joe Bailon is famous for inventing the paint color "Candy Apple Red" in 1956. It took Bailon ten years to find the right mix of paints for the color.

Today, the paint jobs of many cars contain shimmer and other effects directly from the factory. As a result, many custom painters focus on decorating vehicles with images and designs.

An Art Form

During the 1950s, custom painters began pinstriping vehicles. Pinstriping involves painting thin lines along cars' bodies to accentuate their shapes. Custom painters also use pinstripes to create intricate decorations. **Graphics**, such as lettering and images, became popular during this time. Scallops, a design originally painted on airplanes and race cars in the 1930s, also became a popular design to paint on vehicles. Today, many custom cars feature hand-painted or **airbrushed** images, including flames, lightning bolts, and cultural and religious symbols, such as national flags and crosses. These images may be painted on the cars, or applied with decals and magnetic stick-ons.

(above) Many custom painters pinstripe, or paint very thin lines, on vehicles. Pinstriping began in the 1950s, but remains a popular car design today.

(below) Scallops are painted on a vehicle to suggest that it reaches top speeds.

Celebrity Car Culture

Celebrities often define what is "cool" and popular. The cars they drive are considered to have street cred. Their cars are trendsetting, which means that they establish trends, or fads, that other people follow.

Cars and Music

The music industry has helped to create cool car culture. Many hip-hop artists own street cred cars, which display their wealth and style. They use flashy custom cars in their music videos to increase their street cred. Displaying cool cars and car accessories in music videos also acts as advertising for the companies that manufacture and sell them. For example, rap videos and song lyrics have helped to increase the sales of a type of rim known as "dubs," or "deuce zeros." Dubs are 20 inches (51 centimeters) in diameter and are made of chrome or aluminum.

(above) Cars with street cred are important status symbols in the hip-hop community. Hip hop music artist Ludacris performs at the 2005 Black Entertainment Television awards ceremony.

The members of the hip-hop music group Black Eyed Peas helped Honda promote a new model by giving away a customized car, which the group helped design.

28

(above) Car designer and builder Dean Bryant customized a 1950 Mercury for the movie, Gone in 60 Seconds. *The car's exhaust pipes shoot out flames.*

(below) Car customizer George Barris customized this 1967 Pontiac GTO for the movie XXX.

Movie Rides

Movies have helped develop cool car culture since the 1950s. When seen on the movie screen, street cred cars attract the attention of car enthusiasts in the audience. In 1955, a hot rod race was featured in the movie *Rebel Without a Cause*. The race appealed to many teenagers, and promoted racing hot rods on city streets across America. The 2001 movie *The Fast and the Furious* was set in Los Angeles and tells a story of tuner racers. The movie helped make tuner racing more popular. Fast and cool street cred cars are still featured in movies today.

Behind the Machines

Innovative people are behind every custom car. Hot rods, fast tuners, and other vehicles with street cred would not exist if there were not people dedicating their careers to making cool cars.

George Barris

Custom car designer George Barris is considered one of the best designers in the world. He is commonly called the "King of Kustomizers." He customized his first car, a 1925 Buick, with his brother Sam. They formed a customizing business in California called Barris Kustom Industries, building race cars and custom vehicles for private buyers. Their work soon attracted the attention of movie studios, and they began creating cars for films and movie stars. George Barris's cars have won many awards, and have been featured in television programs, movies, and commercials.

Ed Bergenholtz

Ed Bergenholtz is considered one of the fastest tuner racers in the United States. Bergenholtz competes in drag races organized by the National Hot Rod Association (NHRA). As a teenager, Bergenholtz raced cars on city streets in California. He first raced in the NHRA series in a Honda CRX that he and his brother Ron tuned. In the 2004 Sport Compact World Finals, Bergenholtz set a world record when he sped down the strip in less than eight seconds. He raced in a Mazda6, and achieved a speed of about 184 miles per hour (296 kilometers per hour).

In 1966, the "King of Kustomizers," George Barris, designed and built the famous Bat Bike and Batmobile for the television series "Batman."

Boyd Coddington

In the early days of building hot rods, car owners rarely hired others to build their hot rods for them. In 1978, Boyd Coddington opened a car shop where he designed and built hot rods for customers. Coddington was also the first manufacturer to create a car wheel from a billet, or chunk, of aluminum. Coddington has built more than 300 hot rods, which have been featured in car shows, museums, and television programs. He has won several awards for his hot rod designs, including the America's Most Beautiful Roadster award for his car called the Boydster. Coddington continues to design and build hot rods today, and manufactures custom wheels from his shop in California.

Ed "Big Daddy" Roth

Ed Roth, nicknamed "Big Daddy", was a hot rod builder in California. Roth's hot rods are considered works of art among hot rod fans. He was one of the first builders to construct car bodies from **fiberglass**. Ed Roth was also an artist and cartoonist, who drew pictures of characters driving hot rods. His most famous cartoon character is a rat named Rat Fink. Images of Rat Fink have been featured on many hot rods. Ed Roth died in 2001.

Boyd Coddington stripped a 1957 Chevrolet Bel Air to create this car, which he named the CheZoom. The CheZoom features Coddington's famous billet aluminum wheels.

Rat Fink, a character created by Ed Roth, became a popular figure featured on hot rods and hot rodding paraphernalia during the 1950s and 1960s.

Glossary

airbrush A device that uses compressed air to spray a liquid, such as paint, onto a surface

alloy A mixture of two or more metals

axle A long bar on which wheels turn

chrome A shiny coating of the metal chromium

coupe A two-door car with a roof

customize To make adjustments to a car to suit the owner's taste

decal A design that is applied to a surface

digital A device that reads, writes, or stores information in numerical form

fiberglass A material made of fine strands of glass

frame A structure that supports or shapes something

front-wheel drive A system whereby only the front wheels of a vehicle receive power from the engine

gearshift A device for changing from one gear to another in a car's transmission

graphics Artwork applied to a vehicle's surface

hubcap A round covering over the hub, or central part, of a wheel

hydraulic Machinery operated by a liquid, especially water

import To buy goods from another country

magnetic Able to attract iron and steel

plated Coated with a thin layer of metal, such as chromium

salt flat A flat area of land covered in salt left by a water body that once covered the land

sport utility vehicle A large vehicle that has four-wheel drive and is designed for off-road travel

slang Informal vocabulary made up of invented or changed words, and exaggerated or funny figures of speech

suede Leather with a soft, velvety surface

supercharger A mechanical device that forces more air-fuel mixture into an engine to increase its performance

transmission Gears and other car parts that transmit, or send, power from the engine to the wheels

tweed A coarse woolen fabric

upholstery The soft padded covering that is fixed to furniture, such as car seats

vanity license plate A license plate that contains numbers and letters that form a word, such as a name, or phrase

Index

Acura 9, 10
aftermarket parts 5, 14, 16, 18, 24

Bailon, Joe 26
Barris, George 29, 30
Bergenholtz, Ed 30

California 4, 6, 7, 9, 13, 30, 31
car competitions 5, 18, 25
car shows 5, 12, 13, 19, 31
Chevrolet 6, 7, 10, 12, 21, 31
Chevrolet Impala 10
CheZoom 31
Coddington, Boyd 31
concept cars 19, 20

cruising 4, 6, 8, 10
customizing 5, 11, 13, 16-19, 20, 22-23, 24, 26-27, 28, 29, 30

Detroit 8
Dodge 7, 8, 10, 12
drag race 7, 8, 9, 13, 14, 15, 29, 30

engine 5, 7, 9, 12, 13, 14, 15, 17

Ford 6, 7, 8, 10, 12, 14

global positioning system 21

hip-hop 23, 28

Honda 9, 10, 12, 14, 19, 28, 30
Honda Civic 9, 10, 12, 14, 15
hot rod 5, 7, 12-13, 29, 30, 31
hydraulic suspension 10

Japan 9, 14, 19

lighting 11, 13, 18, 21
lowrider 4, 6, 10-11

Mazda 9, 10, 12, 14, 30
Mercury 7, 12, 29

National Hot Rod Association 13, 14, 30

Nissan 9, 10, 14

paint 7, 11, 13, 14, 16, 26-27
pinstriping 27

rims 14, 22, 23, 28
Roth, Ed 31

spoilers 14, 15, 18
stereo systems 4, 11, 14, 20, 24-25

Toyota 5, 10, 14, 24
tuner 5, 9, 14-15, 29, 30

Woodward Avenue 8

Printed in the U.S.A.